The Roar Is Love

The Roar Is Love: Harvest Journal

Copyright © 2021 Brandi Caldwell-Harris

All rights reserved. No part of this book may be used or reproduced by any means, graphic, electronic, mechanical, including photocopying, recording, taping, or by any information storage retrieval system without the prior written permission of the publisher. The only exception is brief quotations in printed reviews.

Unless otherwise indicated, scripture quotations marked KJV are taken from the King James Version of the Holy Bible.

Scripture quotations identified NIV taken from the Holy Bible: International Standard Version®. Copyright © 1973, 1978, 1984 Biblica. Used by permission of Zondervan. All rights reserved.

Scripture quotations identified AMPC taken from the Amplified® Bible (AMPC), Copyright © 1954, 1958, 1962, 1964, 1965, 1987 by The Lockman Foundation. Used by permission.

Scripture quotations identified NKJV are taken from the New King James Version. Copyright © 1982 by Thomas Nelson, Inc. Used by permission. All rights reserved.

ISBN: 978-0-578-88922-1

A Publication of Rane Publishing, La Vergne, TN

Cover design and editing by Rane Publishing, La Vergne, TN

Printed in the United States of America

The Roar Is Love

Harvest Journal

Brandi Caldwell-Harris

Rane Publishing

DEDICATIONS

I dedicate this book to Jesus, who empowered me with His love, and gave me the opportunity for so many incredible encounters to see a harvest of souls.

I also dedicate this book to my sons: Cameron, River, and Cass. You are truly the best gifts I have ever received from Jesus. I pray that you know the love of Jesus deeply, and that you never let the cares of this world dim your shine. You were born to run your race, so run! I thank God for choosing me to be your Momma, and a BB to my beautiful grandbabies.

- Love, Mom

ACKNOWLEDGMENTS

I want to thank my amazing helpmate and life partner, my husband, who has loved me like Jesus loves the church. Through all my imperfections, he pushes me, counsels me, prays for me, encourages me, makes me laugh, and is my best friend. I couldn't be more thankful that God brought him into my life.

To my mentors and friends: I want to personally thank you for helping me on my journey with Jesus. I am the person I am today because you stopped for me in some way. Your time and effort is noted in Heaven, and many souls know the love of Jesus because of your "yes!" I love you all so much.

TABLE OF CONTENTS

Introduction	A Letter from the Author	1
Day 1	Compel Them to Come	4
Day 2	The Words of Love Mentors	6
Day 3	How Beautiful Are the Feet	8
Day 4	He Walks With Me	10
Day 5	My Name is Jewel	12
Day 6	The Kite	14
Day 7	Chariots of Fire	16
Day 8	My Prize Possessions	18
Day 9	Childlike Faith	20
Day 10	First Responders	22
Day 11	Whoop Whoop	24
Day 12	It Is A Matter of Life or Death	26
Day 13	Dum-Dums Sucker	28
Day 14	My Son, the Dreamer	30
Day 15	Unsung Heroes	32
Day 16	The Friendship of Jesus	34
Day 17	A Letter to My Sunflower	36
Day 18	I Can't Live Without Your Presence	38
Day 19	A Mother's Cry	40
Day 20	Grape Kool-Aid	44
Day 21	Love Encounter	46
End Notes	A Love Letter to Laborers	48
	Closing Statement	49
	A Call to Salvation	50
	Share Your Harvest Stories	51
	About the Author	66

Author's Note

I grew up in a small town with a huge personality, and big dreams. I remember running into a friend of mine, in the middle of the road, and exclaiming all my dreams to him at 100 words per minute. With wide eyes, they said, "You have a gregarious personality. You were born for something great. You could be famous."

God gave me many opportunities in my life to show compassion towards others. I grew up with parents who had fallen to addiction, and took their own lives at a very young age. I also lost my sisters, not to the spirit of death, but to the lifestyle that the spirit of addiction entangled them in.

The Encounter: I was in a moment of desperation, feeling the fork in the road of life and death, as I cried out to God from my jail cell. I felt liquid love seep into the depths of my very being. Although the cell is dark and gloomy in the natural, in the spirit, it was as if the Sun was beaming on my face for over an hour. This encounter changed my life forever. He showed up in my darkest moment to show me that I have always been loved by Him. God showed me how He would resurrect a great love army from the broken and desolate places. These people would be used mightily for His glory. Now, 13 years later, I have watched as many souls have returned to His loving arms. His greatest desire is for His people to know His love. I see the multitudes rising for His great love army.

Through the power of His love, I have also encountered Elyashib - the God who restores. The love that He has poured over me became a witness to my family. He is redeeming the time for me and my children, and mended our hearts for one another in the most beautiful ways.

This is not the final chapter of my story. I have many souls (jewels) to add to God's jewelry box. My heart for this journal is that the laborers never stop or give up, and that the harvest responds to testimony.

Jesus, make our feet beautiful.

"And how shall they preach, except they be sent? as it is written, How beautiful are the feet of them that preach the gospel of peace, and bring glad tidings of good things!"
Romans 10:15 KJV

"And he had in his right hand seven stars: and out of his mouth went a sharp two-edged sword: and his countenance was as the sun shineth in his strength."
Revelations 1:16 KJV

#THEROARISLOVE

Day One

"Compel Them to Come"

We are living in a time similar to Luke 14:23 (NIV) – "Then the master told his servant, 'Go out to the roads and country lanes and compel them to come in, so that my house will be full.'"

My heart for today: May you wake up to the love of Jesus, and allow Him to fill you with a fresh passion and desire for souls. Don't waste a single day, and always love the one in front of you.

#theroarislove

A Time of Reflection...

What did the Lord minister to you through today's devotion?

_____
_____
_____
_____
_____
_____
_____

What are your prayers & scriptures today for the harvest?

_____
_____
_____
_____
_____
_____
_____

Day Two

"The Words of Love Mentors"

I'm very grateful for the mentors that the Lord has placed in my path. I want to share some words of wisdom that have been imparted to me, and tattooed on my heart. "Love is the only thing you will lay your life down for." In other words, religion won't do it. Tradition won't do it. Intimacy with the Father, and knowing the true love of God, will always propel you to give your resounding yes.

Another statement that has always stuck with me is, "The greatest love story ever told is what Jesus did on the cross." God is love. Love covers a multitude of sins. I pray you come to know the fullness of His love, and allow Him to pour that into you.

#theroarislove

A Time of Reflection...

What did the Lord minister to you through today's devotion?

_____
_____
_____
_____
_____
_____
_____
_____

What are your prayers & scriptures today for the harvest?

_____
_____
_____
_____
_____
_____
_____
_____

Day Three

"How Beautiful Are the Feet?"

His Word exclaims how beautiful are the feet that bring the good news? Our heart cry should scream, "Give me souls for my inheritance." Many years ago, I was incarcerated for a drug charge. The Lord started to break my heart for the broken and the lost. I would sit at the feet of women and listen to their stories of horror and pain. I began to feel His love for His people. He said to me, "Don't ever waste an opportunity to make my name known. My desire is that they truly know how loved they are by me." I'm so grateful that He broke my heart for the harvest. I'm undone by His love. My prayer is that you ask Him to do the same in your life, and make your feet beautiful.

#theroarislove

A Time of Reflection...

What did the Lord minister to you through today's devotion?

___

What are your prayers & scriptures today for the harvest?

___

Day Four

"He Walks With Me"

I had a dream that an angel sat a music box on my chest. When it opened, the song "He Walks With Me," began to play. The lyrics flowed from the box and penetrated my heart. I heard, "He walks with me, and He talks with me, and He tells me I am His own." When I woke up from the dream, I was overwhelmed with the thought that we are never alone. He is always with us, reminding us, that we are His very own. Jesus will never leave you nor forsake you.

A Time of Reflection…

What did the Lord minister to you through today's devotion?

_____
_____
_____
_____
_____
_____
_____
_____

What are your prayers & scriptures today for the harvest?

_____
_____
_____
_____
_____
_____
_____
_____

Day Five

"My Name is Jewel"

I was walking on a sunny day, and I began to feel discouraged. I started to ask the Lord if I was even making a difference. For years, I believed if you stopped for the one He placed in front of you, an army would arise. As I walked up my steps, He placed "the one" right in front of me. The Lord gently said, "She feels voiceless. Just sit and listen." I see every lost soul as a jewel, or diamond, that God wants to add to His jewelry box. She began to share with me her long life of pain. She walked through dark seasons which included prostitution, drugs, and dancing in the night. As she was talking, I felt the love of God and His compassion for His people. When she finished sharing her story, I asked for her name. She said my stage name is, "Diamond," but my Father named me "Jewel." I began to weep, as the Lord was showing His faithfulness in stopping for the one, and collecting His jewels. We are all so valuable to Him, and that will never change. Valuable is defined as extremely useful or important, and something of great worth. He placed His worth on the inside of us, and He is calling us to see the treasure on the inside of each person we encounter.

17 And they shall be Mine, says the Lord of hosts, in that day when I publicly recognize and openly declare them to be My jewels (My special possession, My peculiar treasure). And I will spare them, as a man spares his own son who serves him.

Malachi 3:17 AMPC

#theroarislove

A Time of Reflection…

What did the Lord minister to you through today's devotion?

_____
_____
_____
_____
_____
_____
_____
_____

What are your prayers & scriptures today for the harvest?

_____
_____
_____
_____
_____
_____
_____
_____

Day Six

"The Kite"

Have you ever thought about how free flowing a kite is? They move along with the wind, but they are still connected to a source. I want to share with you a vision that the Lord gave me regarding kites. The Father was standing at the end of many kite strings, and he held them all in His hands. Each kite was unique, and made up of beautiful and vibrant colors. I heard Him say, "These are all mine. Celebrate how I made them, and always BE LOVE."

He is very proud of all of His kites that He handpicked to be connected to Him. Each one is born of the winds of the Spirit (John 3:8), and allow Him to freely move them. No matter what it may look like, they abide in Him. The more the Father releases, the higher the kite soars. The string cannot be broken as it has been built through trust, and a loving intimate relationship with Him.

4 *Abide in Me, and I in you. As the branch cannot bear fruit of itself, unless it abides in the vine, neither can you, unless you abide in Me.* 5 *"I am the vine, you are the branches. He who abides in Me, and I in him, bears much fruit; for without Me you can do nothing.* -John 15:4-5 NKJV

#theroarislove

A Time of Reflection...

What did the Lord minister to you through today's devotion?

_____
_____
_____
_____
_____
_____
_____
_____
_____

What are your prayers & scriptures today for the harvest?

_____
_____
_____
_____
_____
_____
_____
_____

Day Seven

"Chariots of Fire"

In 1981, a movie was made in honor of men who were incredible Olympic runners. God showed me that he was releasing the chariots of fire, born to run a race, and pushed by His winds. Not by might, nor by power, but they will move by His spirit. The radical wild runners will run side by side, with a pure flame of love for the Father and for souls. May we always hear His sound to run our race. We will be the burning ones, consumed and possessed by His love, and called to greatness.

13 Brothers and sisters, I do not consider myself yet to have taken hold of it. But one thing I do: Forgetting what is behind and straining toward what is ahead, 14 I press on toward the goal to win the prize for which God has called me heavenward in Christ Jesus.

Philippians 3:13-14 NIV

A Time of Reflection...

What did the Lord minister to you through today's devotion?

_____
_____
_____
_____
_____
_____
_____
_____

What are your prayers & scriptures today for the harvest?

_____
_____
_____
_____
_____
_____
_____

Day Eight

"My Prize Possession"

I had a vision of a jewelry box. Jesus opened the box, picked the jewels up, and breathed on them.

These jewels were so precious to him. We get to co-labor with love to put His jewels in His treasure box.

Clothed in God's glory [in all its splendor and radiance]. The luster of it resembled a rare and most precious jewel, like jasper, shining clear as crystal.
Revelation 21:11 AMPC

Let this be your declaration: God send me, I'll go!

A Time of Reflection...

What did the Lord minister to you through today's devotion?

_____
_____
_____
_____
_____
_____
_____
_____

What are your prayers & scriptures today for the harvest?

_____
_____
_____
_____
_____
_____
_____
_____

Day Nine

"Childlike Faith"

I was in a season where I was surrounded by children. I knew I was called to kids during this time. I would hear, "Let the little children come."

In that moment, God was showing me that He also wanted restore childlike faith to people who had grown weary in the harvest field for souls. Childlike faith attracts His presence, and miracles take place. Don't ever lose your childlike faith. The harvest needs you.

#theroarislove

A Time of Reflection...

What did the Lord minister to you through today's devotion?

What are your prayers & scriptures today for the harvest?

Day Ten

"First Responders"

My sisters in Christ and I were test driving a car for me. It was a beautiful sunny day. We were at a stop sign when we heard gun shots, and just like that, we were called to be first responders. People began to scatter in fear, as this man with blood seeping from his body began to scream, "I've been shot! Someone help me!" No one moved. I started screaming, "Call 911!" We ran over to him, and I couldn't help but notice that everyone else was still just standing there. We leaned him on a car. One sister held his bloody wound and began to pray. My other sister was calling for help. I recall asking him if he knew Jesus. He was crying out for his natural father that had passed away. "He cannot help you," I said, "The power of Jesus is what we need right now." I started to pray with him. God saved his life that day. We all went to see him, and he expressed his deepest gratitude. We also got the opportunity to pray for his family. Lives were changed in response to the call. God is looking for first responders who will be fearless for souls. How will you respond to the call?

A Time of Reflection...

What did the Lord minister to you through today's devotion?

_____
_____
_____
_____
_____
_____
_____
_____

What are your prayers & scriptures today for the harvest?

_____
_____
_____
_____
_____
_____
_____

Day Eleven

"Whoop, Whoop"

What a wild title for an entry, right? Let me explain.

My good friends from Illinois said they knew an outreach that would be right up my alley. They know my heart for the outcasts. So, I said, yes. I couldn't wait to go find some of the Lord's jewels. There is a band called Insane Clown Posse. Their fans are called Juggalos. Every time they would pass one another, you would hear, "Whoop, whoop!" Whoop, whoop means, "Hi family, glad you're here." Kids and adults come from all over the world to spend a week dressing like clowns, partaking in drugs and alcohol, and enjoying the music. Honestly, it was one of the darkest places that I have ever been. I was overwhelmed as I watched thousands of people that did not know the true love of Jesus. They had no idea that they could belong to the best family in the Universe – God's family. So, I made it my mission to share Jesus every chance I got.

I recall one girl who was overdosing in my arms. I cried out to the Lord, and He saved her that day. She was filled with the precious gift of the Holy Spirit.

Jesus, help us to bring your kids home to a safe family.

#theroarislove

A Time of Reflection...

What did the Lord minister to you through today's devotion?

_____
_____
_____
_____
_____
_____
_____
_____
_____

What are your prayers & scriptures today for the harvest?

_____
_____
_____
_____
_____
_____
_____
_____

Day Twelve

"It is a Matter of Life or Death That We Go"

My husband shared a story with me about a young boy that he was incarcerated with. At this time, he knew Jesus was real, but he had not completely surrendered to the Lord. He heard the voice of the Lord, and he told him to share the good news with this young man. He was scared, but God would not leave him alone. He finally ministered to this young man, and he was saved. One week later, the guard handed my husband a newspaper. He saw a story about that same young man. He was released from jail, and passed away in a car accident. So, again I say, it's a matter of life and death. Who will go?

A Time of Reflection...

What did the Lord minister to you through today's devotion?

_____
_____
_____
_____
_____
_____
_____
_____

What are your prayers & scriptures today for the harvest?

_____
_____
_____
_____
_____
_____
_____

Day Thirteen

"Dum-Dums Sucker"

I love suckers, and made sure to share them on every outreach. My husband and I moved from Kentucky to Ohio on assignment. We were riding our bikes through the neighborhood, and I noticed a painting of Dum-Dums Suckers. I discovered that they were founded here. As we continued our ride, I reflected on the countless suckers that I gave to God's kids. I knew that He was reminding me of His love for the harvest. Then, my neighbor surprised me with a bag of suckers. He actually works for the company. I was so excited. It was another sign from the Father, so I asked God what He was saying. He responded with, "It's harvest time. I'm going to release my sweetness to people who have never tasted and seen that I am good." He speaks to us in many ways if we have eyes to see, and ears to hear.

[8] *O taste and see that the LORD is good: blessed is the man that trusteth in him.*
Psalms 34:8 KJV

Tell someone of His goodness today.

#theroarislove

A Time of Reflection...

What did the Lord minister to you through today's devotion?

_____
_____
_____
_____
_____
_____
_____
_____

What are your prayers & scriptures today for the harvest?

_____
_____
_____
_____
_____
_____
_____

Day Fourteen

"My Son, the Dreamer"

I woke up one morning, and my youngest son began to share a dream that he had. He said, "Momma, all of these people were asking me, "Which way do I go?"" He responded, "My Mom says to walk in love." He described a huge heart that God showed Him in the dream, and multitudes of people were walking toward it.

My son was 11 years old at that time. Today, I understand with clarity that love is the key, and we need to make that our main focus. We will lead people into the heart of God's love. Later that day, my son drew a picture of a lion, and it was roaring. That's when I heard, "The Roar is Love."

Perfect love cast out all fear.

I pray that you understand God's perfect love for you. Ask Him to fill you to the overflow with His love, so it will ooze from your life into the harvest of His people.

#theroarislove

A Time of Reflection...

What did the Lord minister to you through today's devotion?

_____
_____
_____
_____
_____
_____
_____
_____

What are your prayers & scriptures today for the harvest?

_____
_____
_____
_____
_____
_____
_____

Day Fifteen

"Unsung Heroes"

One Summer Day, my friend asked me if I would come to a cookout. I wasn't going to go because I didn't know any of the other people that were going to be there. Then, I heard the voice of the Lord tell me to go. So, I went. When I arrived, I got some snacks and waited for instruction from the Lord.

All of a sudden, a woman came sprinting down the alley. God said, "I sent you for her, go!" I began to chase her with my watermelon in one hand, and my Mountain Dew in the other. She was yelling that someone had stolen her car. I knew that she was telling the truth, but I could also discern that she was very high. When I got close, she dropped to the ground like a rock. She was out cold. I heard a gentle voice say, "Bind the spirit of death or she will die here today." I bent over, and cut the head off of that spirit. Immediately, her eyes popped open. As police arrived on the scene, I quietly backed away.

God is looking for unsung heroes who will obey His voice, and stop for the one. Declaration: <u>Let that be You in me</u>.

#theroarislove

A Time of Reflection...

What did the Lord minister to you through today's devotion?

_____
_____
_____
_____
_____
_____
_____
_____

What are your prayers & scriptures today for the harvest?

_____
_____
_____
_____
_____
_____
_____

Day Sixteen

"The Friendship of Jesus"

Amelia Earhart was a woman who embraced the pioneering spirit in her time. She carried a big dream during the 20's. She desired to be an aviator in a time when it was a man's world. To say that it would was easy is an understatement. The name of her plane was highlighted to me, as I watched the first time she crossed the Pacific Ocean. It was called friendship.

This caused me to meditate on the friendship of Jesus, and how important it is that we understand it. I was immediately reminded of this scripture, "Jesus sticks closer than a brother." We are truly living in a time that knowing Jesus as friend is very important. We need to co-labor with Him, in the harvest fields, in order to navigate through the turbulence that life can bring. We will be like Amelia who bravely broke through barriers that tried to keep her grounded. So, run with the friendship of God. It's so worth it. I say to you, don't stay grounded. You were born to soar in the clouds with your friend, Jesus.

[24] A man that hath friends must shew himself friendly: and there is a friend that sticketh closer than a brother. - Proverbs 18:24 KJV

#theroarislove

A Time of Reflection...

What did the Lord minister to you through today's devotion?

___

What are your prayers & scriptures today for the harvest?

___

Day Seventeen

"A Letter to My Sunflower"

Those that look to me will never be put to shame, and their faces will be radiant. Just as a sunflower turns its face to the sunlight in My Heavens, you are called to keep your face towards my Son, Jesus. His countenance will rest upon you as you gaze upon Him. His glory will rest upon you as you rest in Him. May you behold the beauty of His splendor by gazing into His eyes.
I bless you to SHINE with the light of His presence, and to love all of your days.

[25] *The Lord make His face to shine upon and enlighten you and be gracious (kind, merciful, and giving favor) to you;*
Numbers 6:25 AMPC

A Time of Reflection...

What did the Lord minister to you through today's devotion?

_____
_____
_____
_____
_____
_____
_____
_____

What are your prayers & scriptures today for the harvest?

_____
_____
_____
_____
_____
_____
_____
_____

Day Eighteen

"I Can't Live Without Your Presence"

A few weeks after we moved to Ohio, I was awakened one night around 2:30 A.M. For a couple of hours, all I could hear was, "I can't live without Your presence." The Lord sang it over and over to me. The next day, I went for a ride on my bike to pray. The Lord said, "I'm calling a company of people who do not want to live without my presence. They must feast from the Bread of Life. They are undone."

A Time of Reflection...

What did the Lord minister to you through today's devotion?

_____
_____
_____
_____
_____
_____
_____
_____

What are your prayers & scriptures today for the harvest?

_____
_____
_____
_____
_____
_____
_____
_____

Day Nineteen

"A Mother's Cry"

The poem you are about to read was birthed out of a desperate cry for her sons who had been taken captive by the monster of addiction. I love and honor my mother-in-law greatly. She is a very courageous woman who knows how to pray. My husband today is sober and leading many to that same hope in Jesus. I dedicate this poem to all the moms who are crying out for their children.

An Addict's Mother's Prayer

It is 3:00 A.M. and most are asleep,

But the addict's mother lays there with thoughts so deep.

You don't see her tears, or hear her softly pray,

Nor do you hear what the Lord hears her say.

Father PLEASE hear my please,

As the tears flow down her cheeks,

It is for my son Lord, Your peace that I seek.

Satan has him fooled, and drugs have led him astray,

Lord please have mercy on him today.

Then she wonders just where he is tonight,

And the truth only brings her sickness and fright.

Then with even more passion she earnestly prays,

Please Father just let him live another day!

Open his eyes so that he might see,

You are the only One that can set him free.

I know you have angels that watch over him,

I beg of you Lord, please don't let Satan win.

In Jesus precious name, I pray, Amen!

-Karen Jo Kirby

A Time of Reflection...

What did the Lord minister to you through today's devotion?

_____
_____
_____
_____
_____
_____
_____
_____

What are your prayers & scriptures today for the harvest?

_____
_____
_____
_____
_____
_____
_____
_____

Day Twenty

"Grape Kool-Aid"

During my 7 months and 21 days of incarceration, we were frequently served hot dogs and grape Kool-Aid. This contributed to people contracting infections that afflicted our bodies, and I found myself complaining all the time. Then one day, I heard the Lord say, "Do you want this territory?" I said, "Yes!" His response was to praise Him for all of it. Your harvest influence will come by the position of your heart. So, praise Him in ALL things. With my "yes," I've had the honor to go into numerous jails and rehabs, and many souls have been ignited with hope.

[6] But godliness with contentment is great gain. [7] For we brought nothing into this world, and it is certain we can carry nothing out. [8] And having food and raiment let us be therewith content. [9] But they that will be rich fall into temptation and a snare, and into many foolish and hurtful lusts, which drown men in destruction and perdition. [10] For the love of money is the root of all evil: which while some coveted after, they have erred from the faith, and pierced themselves through with many sorrows. [11] But thou, O man of God, flee these things; and follow after righteousness, godliness, faith, love, patience, meekness. [12] Fight the good fight of faith, lay hold on eternal life, whereunto thou art also called, and hast professed a good profession before many witnesses.

1 Timothy 6:6-12 KJV

#theroarislove

A Time of Reflection...

What did the Lord minister to you through today's devotion?

_____

_____

_____

_____

_____

_____

_____

_____

What are your prayers & scriptures today for the harvest?

_____

_____

_____

_____

_____

_____

_____

Day Twenty-One

"Love Encounter"

It was as if the sun was shining just for me. One day, I began to cry out from my jail cell, "Lord, please reveal Your love to me. I am desperate." All of a sudden, I was frozen in the light of His countenance. In a previous verse, Revelations revealed that His countenance is as the Sun. I could not move my body for 45 minutes. Everyone in my cell was supernaturally put to sleep, and I felt liquid love pour through my veins. I could not stop weeping. He showed me His love, and told me that in the last hour, it was the only way. Only pure love will do.

If you have never felt the pure love of God, keep asking Him. A radical love encounter with Him will change your life FOREVER.

#theroarislove

A Time of Reflection...

What did the Lord minister to you through today's devotion?

_____
_____
_____
_____
_____
_____
_____
_____
_____

What are your prayers & scriptures today for the harvest?

_____
_____
_____
_____
_____
_____
_____
_____

A Love Letter to the Laborers

Thank you so much for your "yes" to follow Me. Oh, thank you for being a fisher of men for My kingdom. Thank you for all of the cups of mercy that you show to my sons and daughters. I will always make it worth it. Though the sun seems long and hard at times, keep close to My heart. I will make you a sign and a wonder of My goodness.

- Love,
Father of Kindness

To The Laborer of the Lord

I pray this journal encourages you to love God with all of your heart, and to be love to the one God sets before you. Let's go forth and harvest souls for Jesus, adding to the kingdom, and our inheritance.

- Brandi Caldwell-Harris

Call for Salvation

If you are lost and do not know Jesus, you can come to know Him today.

John 3:16 says, "For God so loved the world that He gave His only begotten Son that whoever believes in Him shall not perish but have everlasting life."

It's really simple. Ask Him into your heart today; ask Him to forgive you, and to lead your life from now on. It will be the greatest adventure of your life!

Share Your Harvest Stories

Document the opportunities and encounters that God has given you to stop for the one.

Share Your Harvest Stories

Document the opportunities and encounters that God has given you to stop for the one.

_____
_____
_____
_____
_____
_____
_____
_____
_____
_____
_____
_____
_____
_____
_____
_____
_____
_____

Share Your Harvest Stories

Document the opportunities and encounters that God has given you to stop for the one.

_____
_____
_____
_____
_____
_____
_____
_____
_____
_____
_____
_____
_____
_____
_____
_____
_____

Share Your Harvest Stories

Document the opportunities and encounters that God has given you to stop for the one.

_____
_____
_____
_____
_____
_____
_____
_____
_____
_____
_____
_____
_____
_____
_____
_____
_____
_____

Share Your Harvest Stories

Document the opportunities and encounters that God has given you to stop for the one.

_____
_____
_____
_____
_____
_____
_____
_____
_____
_____
_____
_____
_____
_____
_____
_____
_____
_____
_____
_____

Share Your Harvest Stories

Document the opportunities and encounters that God has given you to stop for the one.

_____
_____
_____
_____
_____
_____
_____
_____
_____
_____
_____
_____
_____
_____
_____
_____

Share Your Harvest Stories

Document the opportunities and encounters that God has given you to stop for the one.

Share Your Harvest Stories

Document the opportunities and encounters that God has given you to stop for the one.

_____
_____
_____
_____
_____
_____
_____
_____
_____
_____
_____
_____
_____
_____
_____
_____
_____

Share Your Harvest Stories

Document the opportunities and encounters that God has given you to stop for the one.

Share Your Harvest Stories

Document the opportunities and encounters that God has given you to stop for the one.

Share Your Harvest Stories

Document the opportunities and encounters that God has given you to stop for the one.

_____
_____
_____
_____
_____
_____
_____
_____
_____
_____
_____
_____
_____
_____
_____
_____
_____
_____
_____
_____

Share Your Harvest Stories

Document the opportunities and encounters that God has given you to stop for the one.

_____
_____
_____
_____
_____
_____
_____
_____
_____
_____
_____
_____
_____
_____
_____
_____
_____

Share Your Harvest Stories

Document the opportunities and encounters that God has given you to stop for the one.

Share Your Harvest Stories

Document the opportunities and encounters that God has given you to stop for the one.

_____
_____
_____
_____
_____
_____
_____
_____
_____
_____
_____
_____
_____
_____
_____
_____
_____
_____

Share Your Harvest Stories

Document the opportunities and encounters that God has given

you to stop for the one.

_____

_____

_____

_____

_____

_____

_____

_____

_____

_____

_____

_____

_____

_____

_____

_____

About the Author

Brandi Caldwell-Harris is a wife, mother, author, mentor, teacher, prophetic evangelist, BB to her beautiful grandbabies, and the founder of The Roar Is Love Ministry. She co-labors in love, with her husband, Daniel Harris. Brandi is a frontline soldier in God's army, and she has found the most powerful weapon in God's arsenal – LOVE. Through radical encounters with the love of God, she has learned how to stop for the one. She carries the love of God in a way that is indescribable, and she is sure to release what she carries. Brandi's vision is of an army rising, bathed in the love of Jesus, and carrying that torch to all that they encounter. As she passionately pursues God, she also seeks to gather the precious jewels of Heaven to add to His treasure box.

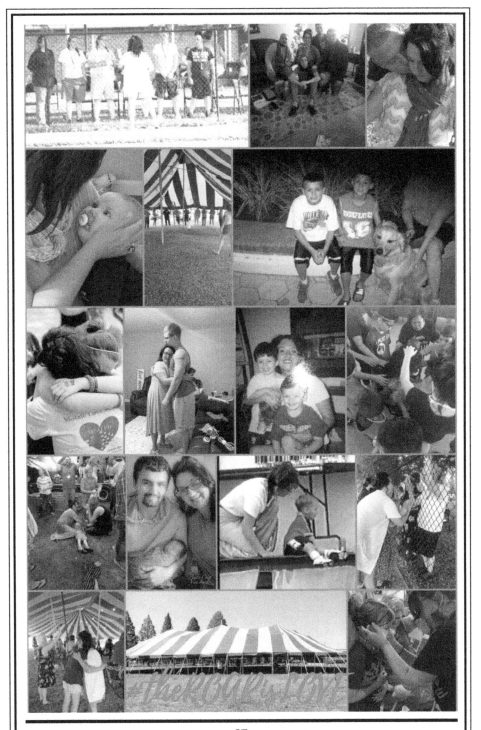

Made in the USA
Monee, IL
02 June 2021